FRACTIONS GRADE 3
MATH ESSENTIALS
Children's Fraction Books

All Rights reserved. No part of this book may be reproduced or used in any way or form or by any means whether electronic or mechanical, this means that you cannot record or photocopy any material ideas or tips that are provided in this book.

Copyright 2016

Enjoy and have fun with Fraction Exercises.

This book belongs to:
_____
Name

Exercise No. 1

Date:

Score:

Compare the following fractions by writing (>, < or =) in each box.

1.) $\frac{2}{3}$ ☐ $\frac{2}{3}$

2.) $\frac{3}{5}$ ☐ $\frac{1}{2}$

3.) $\frac{2}{5}$ ☐ $\frac{3}{5}$

4.) $\frac{5}{6}$ ☐ $\frac{1}{3}$

5.) $\frac{2}{3}$ ☐ $\frac{3}{6}$

6.) $\frac{2}{4}$ ☐ $\frac{3}{4}$

7.) $\frac{1}{2}$ ☐ $\frac{1}{5}$

8.) $\frac{1}{2}$ ☐ $\frac{2}{6}$

9.) $\frac{1}{4}$ ☐ $\frac{2}{4}$

10.) $\frac{2}{4}$ ☐ $\frac{2}{4}$

Exercise No. 2

Date:

Score:

Compare the following fractions by writing (>, < or =) in each box.

1.) $\dfrac{1}{3}$ ☐ $\dfrac{4}{5}$

2.) $\dfrac{5}{6}$ ☐ $\dfrac{4}{5}$

3.) $\dfrac{1}{2}$ ☐ $\dfrac{1}{2}$

4.) $\dfrac{4}{5}$ ☐ $\dfrac{1}{3}$

5.) $\dfrac{2}{3}$ ☐ $\dfrac{1}{6}$

6.) $\dfrac{2}{4}$ ☐ $\dfrac{2}{4}$

7.) $\dfrac{2}{4}$ ☐ $\dfrac{3}{4}$

8.) $\dfrac{2}{6}$ ☐ $\dfrac{1}{2}$

9.) $\dfrac{5}{6}$ ☐ $\dfrac{1}{2}$

10.) $\dfrac{1}{5}$ ☐ $\dfrac{2}{3}$

Exercise No. 3

Date:

Score:

Compare the following fractions by writing (>, < or =) in each box.

1.) $\dfrac{2}{3}$ ☐ $\dfrac{4}{6}$

2.) $\dfrac{1}{4}$ ☐ $\dfrac{2}{4}$

3.) $\dfrac{3}{4}$ ☐ $\dfrac{1}{6}$

4.) $\dfrac{2}{3}$ ☐ $\dfrac{1}{4}$

5.) $\dfrac{3}{5}$ ☐ $\dfrac{5}{6}$

6.) $\dfrac{3}{4}$ ☐ $\dfrac{2}{4}$

7.) $\dfrac{1}{2}$ ☐ $\dfrac{1}{2}$

8.) $\dfrac{1}{3}$ ☐ $\dfrac{1}{2}$

9.) $\dfrac{4}{5}$ ☐ $\dfrac{2}{3}$

10.) $\dfrac{4}{6}$ ☐ $\dfrac{4}{6}$

Exercise No. 4

Date:

Score:

Compare the following fractions by writing (>, < or =) in each box.

1.) $\dfrac{3}{6}$ ☐ $\dfrac{1}{2}$ 6.) $\dfrac{4}{6}$ ☐ $\dfrac{4}{6}$

2.) $\dfrac{4}{5}$ ☐ $\dfrac{2}{3}$ 7.) $\dfrac{2}{3}$ ☐ $\dfrac{1}{3}$

3.) $\dfrac{4}{6}$ ☐ $\dfrac{2}{5}$ 8.) $\dfrac{1}{2}$ ☐ $\dfrac{1}{3}$

4.) $\dfrac{4}{5}$ ☐ $\dfrac{4}{5}$ 9.) $\dfrac{3}{6}$ ☐ $\dfrac{1}{2}$

5.) $\dfrac{3}{4}$ ☐ $\dfrac{1}{5}$ 10.) $\dfrac{1}{2}$ ☐ $\dfrac{2}{4}$

Exercise No. 5

Date:

Score:

Compare the following fractions by writing (>, < or =) in each box.

1.) $\dfrac{2}{5}$ ☐ $\dfrac{2}{6}$ 6.) $\dfrac{3}{6}$ ☐ $\dfrac{4}{5}$

2.) $\dfrac{1}{4}$ ☐ $\dfrac{1}{5}$ 7.) $\dfrac{4}{5}$ ☐ $\dfrac{4}{6}$

3.) $\dfrac{1}{3}$ ☐ $\dfrac{2}{3}$ 8.) $\dfrac{2}{3}$ ☐ $\dfrac{3}{4}$

4.) $\dfrac{1}{3}$ ☐ $\dfrac{1}{2}$ 9.) $\dfrac{2}{5}$ ☐ $\dfrac{2}{6}$

5.) $\dfrac{1}{2}$ ☐ $\dfrac{3}{4}$ 10.) $\dfrac{2}{4}$ ☐ $\dfrac{2}{3}$

Exercise No. 6

Date:

Score:

Compare the following fractions by writing (>, < or =) in each box.

1.) $\dfrac{1}{2}$ ☐ $\dfrac{3}{4}$ 6.) $\dfrac{2}{4}$ ☐ $\dfrac{2}{3}$

2.) $\dfrac{1}{2}$ ☐ $\dfrac{2}{3}$ 7.) $\dfrac{5}{6}$ ☐ $\dfrac{2}{4}$

3.) $\dfrac{1}{2}$ ☐ $\dfrac{3}{6}$ 8.) $\dfrac{2}{6}$ ☐ $\dfrac{1}{2}$

4.) $\dfrac{1}{3}$ ☐ $\dfrac{1}{2}$ 9.) $\dfrac{3}{4}$ ☐ $\dfrac{1}{3}$

5.) $\dfrac{4}{5}$ ☐ $\dfrac{1}{2}$ 10.) $\dfrac{5}{6}$ ☐ $\dfrac{4}{5}$

Exercise No. 7

Date:

Score:

Compare the following fractions by writing (>, < or =) in each box.

1.) $\dfrac{2}{5}$ ☐ $\dfrac{2}{6}$

2.) $\dfrac{1}{4}$ ☐ $\dfrac{1}{5}$

3.) $\dfrac{1}{3}$ ☐ $\dfrac{2}{3}$

4.) $\dfrac{1}{3}$ ☐ $\dfrac{1}{2}$

5.) $\dfrac{1}{2}$ ☐ $\dfrac{3}{4}$

6.) $\dfrac{3}{6}$ ☐ $\dfrac{4}{5}$

7.) $\dfrac{4}{5}$ ☐ $\dfrac{4}{6}$

8.) $\dfrac{2}{3}$ ☐ $\dfrac{3}{4}$

9.) $\dfrac{2}{5}$ ☐ $\dfrac{2}{6}$

10.) $\dfrac{2}{4}$ ☐ $\dfrac{2}{3}$

Exercise No. 8

Date:

Score:

Compare the following fractions by writing (>, < or =) in each box.

1.) $\dfrac{1}{2}$ ☐ $\dfrac{3}{4}$

2.) $\dfrac{1}{2}$ ☐ $\dfrac{2}{3}$

3.) $\dfrac{1}{2}$ ☐ $\dfrac{3}{6}$

4.) $\dfrac{1}{3}$ ☐ $\dfrac{1}{2}$

5.) $\dfrac{4}{5}$ ☐ $\dfrac{1}{2}$

6.) $\dfrac{2}{4}$ ☐ $\dfrac{2}{3}$

7.) $\dfrac{5}{6}$ ☐ $\dfrac{2}{4}$

8.) $\dfrac{2}{6}$ ☐ $\dfrac{1}{2}$

9.) $\dfrac{3}{4}$ ☐ $\dfrac{1}{3}$

10.) $\dfrac{5}{6}$ ☐ $\dfrac{4}{5}$

Exercise No. 9

Date:

Score:

Compare the following fractions by writing (>, < or =) in each box.

1.) $\dfrac{3}{6}$ ☐ $\dfrac{1}{2}$ 6.) $\dfrac{2}{5}$ ☐ $\dfrac{1}{2}$

2.) $\dfrac{2}{4}$ ☐ $\dfrac{1}{4}$ 7.) $\dfrac{5}{6}$ ☐ $\dfrac{2}{3}$

3.) $\dfrac{2}{3}$ ☐ $\dfrac{2}{6}$ 8.) $\dfrac{2}{5}$ ☐ $\dfrac{3}{6}$

4.) $\dfrac{1}{2}$ ☐ $\dfrac{2}{5}$ 9.) $\dfrac{4}{6}$ ☐ $\dfrac{2}{4}$

5.) $\dfrac{3}{5}$ ☐ $\dfrac{1}{2}$ 10.) $\dfrac{2}{4}$ ☐ $\dfrac{1}{3}$

Exercise No. 10

Date:

Score:

Compare the following fractions by writing (>, < or =) in each box.

1.) $\dfrac{2}{4}$ ☐ $\dfrac{2}{3}$ 6.) $\dfrac{2}{4}$ ☐ $\dfrac{1}{3}$

2.) $\dfrac{2}{4}$ ☐ $\dfrac{4}{6}$ 7.) $\dfrac{2}{3}$ ☐ $\dfrac{5}{6}$

3.) $\dfrac{1}{3}$ ☐ $\dfrac{4}{5}$ 8.) $\dfrac{1}{2}$ ☐ $\dfrac{1}{5}$

4.) $\dfrac{2}{5}$ ☐ $\dfrac{2}{3}$ 9.) $\dfrac{1}{2}$ ☐ $\dfrac{1}{4}$

5.) $\dfrac{2}{3}$ ☐ $\dfrac{1}{2}$ 10.) $\dfrac{1}{2}$ ☐ $\dfrac{1}{4}$

Exercise No. 11

Date:

Score:

Compare the following fractions by writing (>, < or =) in each box.

1.) $\dfrac{1}{2}$ ☐ $\dfrac{2}{6}$ 6.) $\dfrac{1}{6}$ ☐ $\dfrac{1}{5}$

2.) $\dfrac{1}{5}$ ☐ $\dfrac{1}{6}$ 7.) $\dfrac{1}{2}$ ☐ $\dfrac{1}{2}$

3.) $\dfrac{3}{6}$ ☐ $\dfrac{2}{3}$ 8.) $\dfrac{2}{4}$ ☐ $\dfrac{5}{6}$

4.) $\dfrac{1}{2}$ ☐ $\dfrac{1}{4}$ 9.) $\dfrac{3}{4}$ ☐ $\dfrac{2}{4}$

5.) $\dfrac{4}{6}$ ☐ $\dfrac{4}{5}$ 10.) $\dfrac{1}{3}$ ☐ $\dfrac{1}{3}$

Exercise No. 12

Date:

Score:

Compare the following fractions by writing (>, < or =) in each box.

1.) $\dfrac{1}{4}$ ☐ $\dfrac{1}{4}$

2.) $\dfrac{2}{5}$ ☐ $\dfrac{4}{5}$

3.) $\dfrac{1}{3}$ ☐ $\dfrac{1}{2}$

4.) $\dfrac{2}{3}$ ☐ $\dfrac{2}{5}$

5.) $\dfrac{2}{3}$ ☐ $\dfrac{2}{3}$

6.) $\dfrac{1}{3}$ ☐ $\dfrac{1}{3}$

7.) $\dfrac{3}{6}$ ☐ $\dfrac{1}{6}$

8.) $\dfrac{3}{4}$ ☐ $\dfrac{2}{4}$

9.) $\dfrac{1}{2}$ ☐ $\dfrac{1}{2}$

10.) $\dfrac{2}{5}$ ☐ $\dfrac{1}{3}$

Exercise No. 13

Date:

Score:

Compare the following fractions by writing (>, < or =) in each box.

1.) $\dfrac{1}{3}$ ☐ $\dfrac{5}{6}$ 6.) $\dfrac{1}{5}$ ☐ $\dfrac{1}{6}$

2.) $\dfrac{2}{5}$ ☐ $\dfrac{3}{6}$ 7.) $\dfrac{3}{5}$ ☐ $\dfrac{1}{4}$

3.) $\dfrac{3}{4}$ ☐ $\dfrac{2}{4}$ 8.) $\dfrac{1}{2}$ ☐ $\dfrac{5}{6}$

4.) $\dfrac{3}{5}$ ☐ $\dfrac{3}{5}$ 9.) $\dfrac{2}{6}$ ☐ $\dfrac{1}{5}$

5.) $\dfrac{1}{6}$ ☐ $\dfrac{2}{4}$ 10.) $\dfrac{2}{3}$ ☐ $\dfrac{4}{5}$

Exercise No. 14

Date:

Score:

Compare the following fractions by writing (>, < or =) in each box.

1.) $\dfrac{1}{2}$ ☐ $\dfrac{1}{2}$ 6.) $\dfrac{2}{3}$ ☐ $\dfrac{4}{5}$

2.) $\dfrac{2}{4}$ ☐ $\dfrac{1}{2}$ 7.) $\dfrac{1}{3}$ ☐ $\dfrac{1}{3}$

3.) $\dfrac{1}{6}$ ☐ $\dfrac{1}{2}$ 8.) $\dfrac{1}{2}$ ☐ $\dfrac{1}{3}$

4.) $\dfrac{3}{4}$ ☐ $\dfrac{1}{4}$ 9.) $\dfrac{2}{4}$ ☐ $\dfrac{2}{3}$

5.) $\dfrac{1}{2}$ ☐ $\dfrac{1}{2}$ 10.) $\dfrac{1}{6}$ ☐ $\dfrac{2}{3}$

Exercise No. 15

Date:

Score:

Write the missing number to complete the equivalent fraction.

1.) $\dfrac{1}{} = \dfrac{6}{30}$

2.) $\dfrac{1}{2} = \dfrac{6}{}$

3.) $\dfrac{9}{12} = \dfrac{}{4}$

4.) $\dfrac{1}{} = \dfrac{6}{36}$

5.) $\dfrac{1}{} = \dfrac{5}{10}$

6.) $\dfrac{8}{12} = \dfrac{}{3}$

7.) $\dfrac{1}{4} = \dfrac{}{20}$

8.) $\dfrac{1}{} = \dfrac{2}{4}$

9.) $\dfrac{}{18} = \dfrac{1}{6}$

10.) $\dfrac{}{4} = \dfrac{9}{12}$

Exercise No. 16

Date:

Score:

Write the missing number to complete the equivalent fraction.

1.) $\dfrac{3}{6} = \dfrac{}{36}$

2.) $\dfrac{}{36} = \dfrac{3}{6}$

3.) $\dfrac{6}{12} = \dfrac{1}{}$

4.) $\dfrac{}{30} = \dfrac{5}{6}$

5.) $\dfrac{}{4} = \dfrac{1}{2}$

6.) $\dfrac{}{30} = \dfrac{1}{5}$

7.) $\dfrac{}{4} = \dfrac{1}{2}$

8.) $\dfrac{}{10} = \dfrac{1}{2}$

9.) $\dfrac{3}{6} = \dfrac{1}{}$

10.) $\dfrac{}{4} = \dfrac{6}{12}$

Exercise No. 17

Date:

Score:

Write the missing number to complete the equivalent fraction.

1.) $\dfrac{16}{24} = \dfrac{4}{}$

2.) $\dfrac{12}{} = \dfrac{3}{6}$

3.) $\dfrac{6}{} = \dfrac{1}{2}$

4.) $\dfrac{4}{6} = \dfrac{24}{}$

5.) $\dfrac{5}{} = \dfrac{1}{2}$

6.) $\dfrac{}{5} = \dfrac{6}{10}$

7.) $\dfrac{}{2} = \dfrac{5}{10}$

8.) $\dfrac{3}{} = \dfrac{18}{24}$

9.) $\dfrac{}{8} = \dfrac{1}{2}$

10.) $\dfrac{3}{} = \dfrac{9}{15}$

Exercise No. 18

Date:

Score:

Write the missing number to complete the equivalent fraction.

1.) $\dfrac{12}{24} = \dfrac{}{6}$

2.) $\dfrac{1}{2} = \dfrac{2}{}$

3.) $\dfrac{10}{} = \dfrac{2}{3}$

4.) $\dfrac{5}{15} = \dfrac{1}{}$

5.) $\dfrac{}{9} = \dfrac{1}{3}$

6.) $\dfrac{}{30} = \dfrac{1}{6}$

7.) $\dfrac{4}{} = \dfrac{2}{3}$

8.) $\dfrac{4}{12} = \dfrac{}{6}$

9.) $\dfrac{}{12} = \dfrac{2}{3}$

10.) $\dfrac{}{6} = \dfrac{1}{2}$

Exercise No. 19

Date:

Score:

Write the missing number to complete the equivalent fraction.

1.) $\dfrac{4}{16} = \dfrac{1}{\_}$

2.) $\dfrac{12}{24} = \dfrac{\_}{4}$

3.) $\dfrac{\_}{18} = \dfrac{1}{3}$

4.) $\dfrac{3}{9} = \dfrac{1}{\_}$

5.) $\dfrac{12}{\_} = \dfrac{3}{4}$

6.) $\dfrac{2}{5} = \dfrac{12}{\_}$

7.) $\dfrac{3}{4} = \dfrac{\_}{20}$

8.) $\dfrac{\_}{36} = \dfrac{3}{6}$

9.) $\dfrac{4}{16} = \dfrac{1}{\_}$

10.) $\dfrac{\_}{18} = \dfrac{1}{6}$

Exercise No. 20

Date:

Score:

Write the missing number to complete the equivalent fraction.

1.) $\dfrac{1}{2} = \dfrac{2}{\_}$

2.) $\dfrac{6}{24} = \dfrac{1}{\_}$

3.) $\dfrac{\_}{15} = \dfrac{3}{5}$

4.) $\dfrac{2}{10} = \dfrac{\_}{5}$

5.) $\dfrac{\_}{20} = \dfrac{3}{4}$

6.) $\dfrac{4}{24} = \dfrac{1}{\_}$

7.) $\dfrac{\_}{12} = \dfrac{5}{6}$

8.) $\dfrac{1}{6} = \dfrac{2}{\_}$

9.) $\dfrac{3}{5} = \dfrac{\_}{25}$

10.) $\dfrac{3}{\_} = \dfrac{6}{8}$

Exercise No. 21

Date:

Score:

Write the missing number to complete the equivalent fraction.

1.) $\dfrac{4}{16} = \dfrac{1}{\_}$

2.) $\dfrac{12}{24} = \dfrac{\_}{4}$

3.) $\dfrac{\_}{18} = \dfrac{1}{3}$

4.) $\dfrac{3}{9} = \dfrac{1}{\_}$

5.) $\dfrac{12}{\_} = \dfrac{3}{4}$

6.) $\dfrac{2}{5} = \dfrac{12}{\_}$

7.) $\dfrac{3}{4} = \dfrac{\_}{20}$

8.) $\dfrac{\_}{36} = \dfrac{3}{6}$

9.) $\dfrac{4}{16} = \dfrac{1}{\_}$

10.) $\dfrac{\_}{18} = \dfrac{1}{6}$

Exercise No. 22

Date:

Score:

Write the missing number to complete the equivalent fraction.

1.) $\dfrac{1}{2} = \dfrac{2}{}$

2.) $\dfrac{6}{24} = \dfrac{1}{}$

3.) $\dfrac{}{15} = \dfrac{3}{5}$

4.) $\dfrac{2}{10} = \dfrac{}{5}$

5.) $\dfrac{}{20} = \dfrac{3}{4}$

6.) $\dfrac{4}{24} = \dfrac{1}{}$

7.) $\dfrac{}{12} = \dfrac{5}{6}$

8.) $\dfrac{1}{6} = \dfrac{2}{}$

9.) $\dfrac{3}{5} = \dfrac{}{25}$

10.) $\dfrac{3}{} = \dfrac{6}{8}$

Exercise No. 23

Date:

Score:

Write the missing number to complete the equivalent fraction.

1.) $\dfrac{\square}{4} = \dfrac{5}{20}$

2.) $\dfrac{10}{\square} = \dfrac{2}{3}$

3.) $\dfrac{\square}{6} = \dfrac{12}{24}$

4.) $\dfrac{\square}{6} = \dfrac{2}{12}$

5.) $\dfrac{6}{8} = \dfrac{\square}{4}$

6.) $\dfrac{\square}{2} = \dfrac{6}{12}$

7.) $\dfrac{4}{\square} = \dfrac{1}{6}$

8.) $\dfrac{2}{3} = \dfrac{4}{\square}$

9.) $\dfrac{3}{5} = \dfrac{\square}{30}$

10.) $\dfrac{2}{\square} = \dfrac{1}{2}$

Exercise No. 24

Date:

Score:

Write the missing number to complete the equivalent fraction.

1.) $\dfrac{1}{\boxed{}} = \dfrac{6}{18}$

2.) $\dfrac{2}{\boxed{}} = \dfrac{10}{15}$

3.) $\dfrac{4}{8} = \dfrac{\boxed{}}{2}$

4.) $\dfrac{\boxed{}}{12} = \dfrac{1}{3}$

5.) $\dfrac{3}{\boxed{}} = \dfrac{18}{30}$

6.) $\dfrac{1}{2} = \dfrac{\boxed{}}{6}$

7.) $\dfrac{1}{6} = \dfrac{5}{\boxed{}}$

8.) $\dfrac{18}{\boxed{}} = \dfrac{3}{5}$

9.) $\dfrac{4}{\boxed{}} = \dfrac{2}{4}$

10.) $\dfrac{2}{4} = \dfrac{\boxed{}}{2}$

Exercise No. 25

Date:

Score:

Write the missing number to complete the equivalent fraction.

1.) $\dfrac{1}{2} = \dfrac{4}{}$

2.) $\dfrac{2}{5} = \dfrac{8}{}$

3.) $\dfrac{}{6} = \dfrac{1}{3}$

4.) $\dfrac{24}{} = \dfrac{4}{5}$

5.) $\dfrac{}{2} = \dfrac{2}{4}$

6.) $\dfrac{9}{} = \dfrac{3}{6}$

7.) $\dfrac{4}{6} = \dfrac{}{36}$

8.) $\dfrac{1}{2} = \dfrac{}{4}$

9.) $\dfrac{4}{5} = \dfrac{}{25}$

10.) $\dfrac{3}{6} = \dfrac{1}{}$

Exercise No. 26

Date:

Score:

Write the missing number to complete the equivalent fraction.

1.) $\dfrac{2}{6} = \dfrac{10}{}$

2.) $\dfrac{5}{10} = \dfrac{1}{}$

3.) $\dfrac{}{3} = \dfrac{5}{15}$

4.) $\dfrac{4}{24} = \dfrac{}{6}$

5.) $\dfrac{4}{6} = \dfrac{}{3}$

6.) $\dfrac{}{15} = \dfrac{2}{3}$

7.) $\dfrac{6}{} = \dfrac{2}{3}$

8.) $\dfrac{4}{16} = \dfrac{1}{}$

9.) $\dfrac{1}{} = \dfrac{2}{4}$

10.) $\dfrac{}{5} = \dfrac{3}{15}$

Exercise No. 27

Date:

Score:

Write the missing number to complete the equivalent fraction.

1.) $\dfrac{}{6} = \dfrac{30}{36}$

2.) $\dfrac{10}{12} = \dfrac{}{6}$

3.) $\dfrac{2}{} = \dfrac{1}{3}$

4.) $\dfrac{2}{4} = \dfrac{}{24}$

5.) $\dfrac{}{5} = \dfrac{3}{15}$

6.) $\dfrac{}{5} = \dfrac{24}{30}$

7.) $\dfrac{3}{} = \dfrac{15}{30}$

8.) $\dfrac{2}{} = \dfrac{4}{10}$

9.) $\dfrac{1}{} = \dfrac{6}{24}$

10.) $\dfrac{6}{} = \dfrac{1}{2}$

Exercise No. 28

Date:

Score:

Write the missing number to complete the equivalent fraction.

1.) $\dfrac{}{36} = \dfrac{1}{6}$

2.) $\dfrac{3}{4} = \dfrac{6}{}$

3.) $\dfrac{4}{10} = \dfrac{2}{}$

4.) $\dfrac{3}{9} = \dfrac{}{3}$

5.) $\dfrac{}{24} = \dfrac{3}{6}$

6.) $\dfrac{3}{4} = \dfrac{15}{}$

7.) $\dfrac{12}{} = \dfrac{3}{5}$

8.) $\dfrac{2}{} = \dfrac{8}{20}$

9.) $\dfrac{}{16} = \dfrac{3}{4}$

10.) $\dfrac{}{4} = \dfrac{2}{8}$

PROGRESS CHART

Write your scores in the table below to see your progress.

Exercise No.	Score	Exercise No.	Score
1		15	
2		16	
3		17	
4		18	
5		19	
6		20	
7		21	
8		22	
9		23	
10		24	
11		25	
12		26	
13		27	
14		28	

Answers

Exercise No. 1

1.) $\frac{2}{3}$ = $\frac{2}{3}$
2.) $\frac{3}{5}$ > $\frac{1}{2}$
3.) $\frac{2}{5}$ < $\frac{3}{5}$
4.) $\frac{5}{6}$ > $\frac{1}{3}$
5.) $\frac{2}{3}$ > $\frac{3}{6}$
6.) $\frac{2}{4}$ < $\frac{3}{4}$
7.) $\frac{1}{2}$ > $\frac{1}{5}$
8.) $\frac{1}{2}$ > $\frac{2}{6}$
9.) $\frac{1}{4}$ < $\frac{2}{4}$
10.) $\frac{2}{4}$ = $\frac{2}{4}$

Exercise No. 2

1.) $\frac{1}{3}$ < $\frac{4}{5}$
2.) $\frac{5}{6}$ > $\frac{4}{5}$
3.) $\frac{1}{2}$ = $\frac{1}{2}$
4.) $\frac{4}{5}$ > $\frac{1}{3}$
5.) $\frac{2}{3}$ > $\frac{1}{6}$
6.) $\frac{2}{4}$ < $\frac{3}{4}$
7.) $\frac{2}{6}$ < $\frac{1}{2}$
8.) $\frac{5}{6}$ > $\frac{1}{2}$
9.) $\frac{1}{5}$ < $\frac{2}{3}$
10.) $\frac{1}{2}$ < $\frac{4}{6}$

Exercise No. 3

1.) $\frac{2}{3}$ = $\frac{4}{6}$
2.) $\frac{1}{4}$ < $\frac{2}{4}$
3.) $\frac{3}{4}$ > $\frac{1}{6}$
4.) $\frac{2}{3}$ > $\frac{1}{4}$
5.) $\frac{3}{5}$ < $\frac{5}{6}$
6.) $\frac{3}{4}$ > $\frac{2}{4}$
7.) $\frac{1}{2}$ = $\frac{1}{2}$
8.) $\frac{1}{3}$ < $\frac{1}{2}$
9.) $\frac{4}{5}$ > $\frac{2}{3}$
10.) $\frac{4}{6}$ = $\frac{4}{6}$

Exercise No. 4

1.) $\frac{3}{6}$ = $\frac{1}{2}$
2.) $\frac{4}{5}$ > $\frac{2}{3}$
3.) $\frac{4}{6}$ > $\frac{2}{5}$
4.) $\frac{4}{5}$ = $\frac{4}{5}$
5.) $\frac{3}{4}$ > $\frac{1}{5}$
6.) $\frac{2}{3}$ > $\frac{1}{3}$
7.) $\frac{1}{2}$ > $\frac{1}{3}$
8.) $\frac{3}{6}$ = $\frac{1}{2}$
9.) $\frac{1}{2}$ = $\frac{2}{4}$
10.) $\frac{1}{2}$ > $\frac{1}{5}$

Answers

Exercise No. 5

1.) $\frac{2}{5}$ $>$ $\frac{2}{6}$ 6.) $\frac{3}{6}$ $<$ $\frac{4}{5}$
2.) $\frac{1}{4}$ $>$ $\frac{1}{5}$ 7.) $\frac{4}{5}$ $>$ $\frac{4}{6}$
3.) $\frac{1}{3}$ $<$ $\frac{2}{3}$ 8.) $\frac{2}{3}$ $<$ $\frac{3}{4}$
4.) $\frac{1}{3}$ $<$ $\frac{1}{2}$ 9.) $\frac{2}{5}$ $>$ $\frac{2}{6}$
5.) $\frac{1}{2}$ $<$ $\frac{3}{4}$ 10.) $\frac{2}{4}$ $<$ $\frac{2}{3}$

Exercise No. 6

1.) $\frac{1}{2}$ $<$ $\frac{3}{4}$ 6.) $\frac{5}{6}$ $>$ $\frac{2}{4}$
2.) $\frac{1}{2}$ $<$ $\frac{2}{3}$ 7.) $\frac{2}{6}$ $<$ $\frac{1}{2}$
3.) $\frac{1}{2}$ $=$ $\frac{3}{6}$ 8.) $\frac{3}{4}$ $>$ $\frac{1}{3}$
4.) $\frac{1}{3}$ $<$ $\frac{1}{2}$ 9.) $\frac{5}{6}$ $>$ $\frac{4}{5}$
5.) $\frac{4}{5}$ $>$ $\frac{1}{2}$ 10.) $\frac{3}{4}$ $>$ $\frac{2}{5}$

Exercise No. 7

1.) $\frac{2}{5}$ $>$ $\frac{2}{6}$ 6.) $\frac{3}{6}$ $<$ $\frac{4}{5}$
2.) $\frac{1}{4}$ $>$ $\frac{1}{5}$ 7.) $\frac{4}{5}$ $>$ $\frac{4}{6}$
3.) $\frac{1}{3}$ $<$ $\frac{2}{3}$ 8.) $\frac{2}{3}$ $<$ $\frac{3}{4}$
4.) $\frac{1}{3}$ $<$ $\frac{1}{2}$ 9.) $\frac{2}{5}$ $>$ $\frac{2}{6}$
5.) $\frac{1}{2}$ $<$ $\frac{3}{4}$ 10.) $\frac{2}{4}$ $<$ $\frac{2}{3}$

Exercise No. 8

1.) $\frac{1}{2}$ $<$ $\frac{3}{4}$ 6.) $\frac{5}{6}$ $>$ $\frac{2}{4}$
2.) $\frac{1}{2}$ $<$ $\frac{2}{3}$ 7.) $\frac{2}{6}$ $<$ $\frac{1}{2}$
3.) $\frac{1}{2}$ $=$ $\frac{3}{6}$ 8.) $\frac{3}{4}$ $>$ $\frac{1}{3}$
4.) $\frac{1}{3}$ $<$ $\frac{1}{2}$ 9.) $\frac{5}{6}$ $>$ $\frac{4}{5}$
5.) $\frac{4}{5}$ $>$ $\frac{1}{2}$ 10.) $\frac{3}{4}$ $>$ $\frac{2}{5}$

Answers

Exercise No. 9

1.) $\frac{3}{6}$ = $\frac{1}{2}$
2.) $\frac{2}{4}$ > $\frac{1}{4}$
3.) $\frac{2}{3}$ > $\frac{2}{6}$
4.) $\frac{1}{2}$ > $\frac{2}{5}$
5.) $\frac{3}{5}$ > $\frac{1}{2}$
6.) $\frac{2}{5}$ < $\frac{1}{2}$
7.) $\frac{5}{6}$ > $\frac{2}{3}$
8.) $\frac{2}{5}$ < $\frac{3}{6}$
9.) $\frac{4}{6}$ > $\frac{2}{4}$
10.) $\frac{2}{4}$ > $\frac{1}{3}$

Exercise No. 10

1.) $\frac{2}{4}$ < $\frac{2}{3}$
2.) $\frac{2}{4}$ < $\frac{4}{6}$
3.) $\frac{1}{3}$ < $\frac{4}{5}$
4.) $\frac{2}{5}$ < $\frac{2}{3}$
5.) $\frac{2}{3}$ > $\frac{1}{2}$
6.) $\frac{2}{3}$ < $\frac{5}{6}$
7.) $\frac{1}{2}$ > $\frac{1}{5}$
8.) $\frac{1}{2}$ > $\frac{1}{4}$
9.) $\frac{1}{2}$ > $\frac{1}{4}$
10.) $\frac{2}{6}$ > $\frac{1}{5}$

Exercise No. 11

1.) $\frac{1}{2}$ > $\frac{2}{6}$
2.) $\frac{1}{5}$ > $\frac{1}{6}$
3.) $\frac{3}{6}$ < $\frac{2}{3}$
4.) $\frac{1}{2}$ > $\frac{1}{4}$
5.) $\frac{4}{6}$ < $\frac{4}{5}$
6.) $\frac{1}{6}$ < $\frac{1}{5}$
7.) $\frac{1}{2}$ = $\frac{1}{2}$
8.) $\frac{2}{4}$ < $\frac{5}{6}$
9.) $\frac{3}{4}$ > $\frac{2}{4}$
10.) $\frac{1}{3}$ = $\frac{1}{3}$

Exercise No. 12

1.) $\frac{1}{4}$ = $\frac{1}{4}$
2.) $\frac{2}{5}$ < $\frac{4}{5}$
3.) $\frac{1}{3}$ < $\frac{1}{2}$
4.) $\frac{2}{3}$ > $\frac{2}{5}$
5.) $\frac{2}{3}$ = $\frac{2}{3}$
6.) $\frac{3}{6}$ > $\frac{1}{6}$
7.) $\frac{3}{4}$ > $\frac{2}{4}$
8.) $\frac{1}{2}$ = $\frac{1}{2}$
9.) $\frac{2}{5}$ > $\frac{1}{3}$
10.) $\frac{1}{5}$ < $\frac{1}{2}$

Answers

Exercise No. 13

1.) $\dfrac{1}{3}\ <\ \dfrac{5}{6}$
2.) $\dfrac{2}{5}\ <\ \dfrac{3}{6}$
3.) $\dfrac{3}{4}\ >\ \dfrac{2}{4}$
4.) $\dfrac{3}{5}\ =\ \dfrac{3}{5}$
5.) $\dfrac{1}{6}\ <\ \dfrac{2}{4}$
6.) $\dfrac{1}{5}\ >\ \dfrac{1}{6}$
7.) $\dfrac{3}{5}\ >\ \dfrac{1}{4}$
8.) $\dfrac{1}{2}\ <\ \dfrac{5}{6}$
9.) $\dfrac{2}{6}\ >\ \dfrac{1}{5}$
10.) $\dfrac{2}{3}\ <\ \dfrac{4}{5}$

Exercise No. 14

1.) $\dfrac{1}{2}\ =\ \dfrac{1}{2}$
2.) $\dfrac{2}{4}\ =\ \dfrac{1}{2}$
3.) $\dfrac{1}{6}\ <\ \dfrac{1}{2}$
4.) $\dfrac{3}{4}\ >\ \dfrac{1}{4}$
5.) $\dfrac{1}{2}\ =\ \dfrac{1}{2}$
6.) $\dfrac{1}{3}\ =\ \dfrac{1}{3}$
7.) $\dfrac{1}{2}\ >\ \dfrac{1}{3}$
8.) $\dfrac{2}{4}\ <\ \dfrac{2}{3}$
9.) $\dfrac{1}{6}\ <\ \dfrac{2}{3}$
10.) $\dfrac{2}{3}\ >\ \dfrac{2}{5}$

Exercise No. 15

1.) $\dfrac{1}{5}\ =\ \dfrac{6}{30}$
2.) $\dfrac{1}{2}\ =\ \dfrac{6}{12}$
3.) $\dfrac{9}{12}\ =\ \dfrac{3}{4}$
4.) $\dfrac{1}{6}\ =\ \dfrac{6}{36}$
5.) $\dfrac{1}{2}\ =\ \dfrac{5}{10}$
6.) $\dfrac{8}{12}\ =\ \dfrac{2}{3}$
7.) $\dfrac{1}{4}\ =\ \dfrac{5}{20}$
8.) $\dfrac{1}{2}\ =\ \dfrac{2}{4}$
9.) $\dfrac{3}{18}\ =\ \dfrac{1}{6}$
10.) $\dfrac{3}{4}\ =\ \dfrac{9}{12}$

Exercise No. 16

1.) $\dfrac{3}{6}\ =\ \dfrac{18}{36}$
2.) $\dfrac{18}{36}\ =\ \dfrac{3}{6}$
3.) $\dfrac{6}{12}\ =\ \dfrac{1}{2}$
4.) $\dfrac{25}{30}\ =\ \dfrac{5}{6}$
5.) $\dfrac{2}{4}\ =\ \dfrac{1}{2}$
6.) $\dfrac{6}{30}\ =\ \dfrac{1}{5}$
7.) $\dfrac{2}{4}\ =\ \dfrac{1}{2}$
8.) $\dfrac{5}{10}\ =\ \dfrac{1}{2}$
9.) $\dfrac{3}{6}\ =\ \dfrac{1}{2}$
10.) $\dfrac{2}{4}\ =\ \dfrac{6}{12}$

Answers

Exercise No. 17

1.) $\dfrac{16}{24} = \dfrac{4}{6}$
2.) $\dfrac{12}{24} = \dfrac{3}{6}$
3.) $\dfrac{6}{12} = \dfrac{1}{2}$
4.) $\dfrac{4}{6} = \dfrac{24}{36}$
5.) $\dfrac{5}{10} = \dfrac{1}{2}$
6.) $\dfrac{3}{5} = \dfrac{6}{10}$
7.) $\dfrac{1}{2} = \dfrac{5}{10}$
8.) $\dfrac{3}{4} = \dfrac{18}{24}$
9.) $\dfrac{4}{8} = \dfrac{1}{2}$
10.) $\dfrac{3}{5} = \dfrac{9}{15}$

Exercise No. 18

1.) $\dfrac{12}{24} = \dfrac{3}{6}$
2.) $\dfrac{1}{2} = \dfrac{2}{4}$
3.) $\dfrac{10}{15} = \dfrac{2}{3}$
4.) $\dfrac{5}{15} = \dfrac{1}{3}$
5.) $\dfrac{3}{9} = \dfrac{1}{3}$
6.) $\dfrac{5}{30} = \dfrac{1}{6}$
7.) $\dfrac{4}{6} = \dfrac{2}{3}$
8.) $\dfrac{4}{12} = \dfrac{2}{6}$
9.) $\dfrac{8}{12} = \dfrac{2}{3}$
10.) $\dfrac{3}{6} = \dfrac{1}{2}$

Exercise No. 19

1.) $\dfrac{4}{16} = \dfrac{1}{4}$
2.) $\dfrac{12}{24} = \dfrac{2}{4}$
3.) $\dfrac{6}{18} = \dfrac{1}{3}$
4.) $\dfrac{3}{9} = \dfrac{1}{3}$
5.) $\dfrac{12}{16} = \dfrac{3}{4}$
6.) $\dfrac{2}{5} = \dfrac{12}{30}$
7.) $\dfrac{3}{4} = \dfrac{15}{20}$
8.) $\dfrac{18}{36} = \dfrac{3}{6}$
9.) $\dfrac{4}{16} = \dfrac{1}{4}$
10.) $\dfrac{3}{18} = \dfrac{1}{6}$

Exercise No. 20

1.) $\dfrac{1}{2} = \dfrac{2}{4}$
2.) $\dfrac{6}{24} = \dfrac{1}{4}$
3.) $\dfrac{9}{15} = \dfrac{3}{5}$
4.) $\dfrac{2}{10} = \dfrac{1}{5}$
5.) $\dfrac{15}{20} = \dfrac{3}{4}$
6.) $\dfrac{4}{24} = \dfrac{1}{6}$
7.) $\dfrac{10}{12} = \dfrac{5}{6}$
8.) $\dfrac{1}{6} = \dfrac{2}{12}$
9.) $\dfrac{3}{5} = \dfrac{15}{25}$
10.) $\dfrac{3}{4} = \dfrac{6}{8}$

Answers

Exercise No. 21

1.) $\dfrac{4}{16} = \dfrac{1}{4}$
2.) $\dfrac{12}{24} = \dfrac{2}{4}$
3.) $\dfrac{6}{18} = \dfrac{1}{3}$
4.) $\dfrac{3}{9} = \dfrac{1}{3}$
5.) $\dfrac{12}{16} = \dfrac{3}{4}$
6.) $\dfrac{2}{5} = \dfrac{12}{30}$
7.) $\dfrac{3}{4} = \dfrac{15}{20}$
8.) $\dfrac{18}{36} = \dfrac{3}{6}$
9.) $\dfrac{4}{16} = \dfrac{1}{4}$
10.) $\dfrac{3}{18} = \dfrac{1}{6}$

Exercise No. 22

1.) $\dfrac{1}{2} = \dfrac{2}{4}$
2.) $\dfrac{6}{24} = \dfrac{1}{4}$
3.) $\dfrac{9}{15} = \dfrac{3}{5}$
4.) $\dfrac{2}{10} = \dfrac{1}{5}$
5.) $\dfrac{15}{20} = \dfrac{3}{4}$
6.) $\dfrac{4}{24} = \dfrac{1}{6}$
7.) $\dfrac{10}{12} = \dfrac{5}{6}$
8.) $\dfrac{1}{6} = \dfrac{2}{12}$
9.) $\dfrac{3}{5} = \dfrac{15}{25}$
10.) $\dfrac{3}{4} = \dfrac{6}{8}$

Exercise No. 23

1.) $\dfrac{1}{4} = \dfrac{5}{20}$
2.) $\dfrac{10}{15} = \dfrac{2}{3}$
3.) $\dfrac{3}{6} = \dfrac{12}{24}$
4.) $\dfrac{1}{6} = \dfrac{2}{12}$
5.) $\dfrac{6}{8} = \dfrac{3}{4}$
6.) $\dfrac{1}{2} = \dfrac{6}{12}$
7.) $\dfrac{4}{24} = \dfrac{1}{6}$
8.) $\dfrac{2}{3} = \dfrac{4}{6}$
9.) $\dfrac{3}{5} = \dfrac{18}{30}$
10.) $\dfrac{2}{4} = \dfrac{1}{2}$

Exercise No. 24

1.) $\dfrac{1}{3} = \dfrac{6}{18}$
2.) $\dfrac{2}{3} = \dfrac{10}{15}$
3.) $\dfrac{4}{8} = \dfrac{1}{2}$
4.) $\dfrac{4}{12} = \dfrac{1}{3}$
5.) $\dfrac{3}{5} = \dfrac{18}{30}$
6.) $\dfrac{1}{2} = \dfrac{3}{6}$
7.) $\dfrac{1}{6} = \dfrac{5}{30}$
8.) $\dfrac{18}{30} = \dfrac{3}{5}$
9.) $\dfrac{4}{8} = \dfrac{2}{4}$
10.) $\dfrac{2}{4} = \dfrac{1}{2}$

Answers

Exercise No. 25

1.) $\dfrac{1}{2} = \dfrac{4}{8}$
2.) $\dfrac{2}{5} = \dfrac{8}{20}$
3.) $\dfrac{2}{6} = \dfrac{1}{3}$
4.) $\dfrac{24}{30} = \dfrac{4}{5}$
5.) $\dfrac{1}{2} = \dfrac{2}{4}$
6.) $\dfrac{9}{18} = \dfrac{3}{6}$
7.) $\dfrac{4}{6} = \dfrac{24}{36}$
8.) $\dfrac{1}{2} = \dfrac{2}{4}$
9.) $\dfrac{4}{5} = \dfrac{20}{25}$
10.) $\dfrac{3}{6} = \dfrac{1}{2}$

Exercise No. 26

1.) $\dfrac{2}{6} = \dfrac{10}{30}$
2.) $\dfrac{5}{10} = \dfrac{1}{2}$
3.) $\dfrac{1}{3} = \dfrac{5}{15}$
4.) $\dfrac{4}{24} = \dfrac{1}{6}$
5.) $\dfrac{4}{6} = \dfrac{2}{3}$
6.) $\dfrac{10}{15} = \dfrac{2}{3}$
7.) $\dfrac{6}{9} = \dfrac{2}{3}$
8.) $\dfrac{4}{16} = \dfrac{1}{4}$
9.) $\dfrac{1}{2} = \dfrac{2}{4}$
10.) $\dfrac{1}{5} = \dfrac{3}{15}$

Exercise No. 27

1.) $\dfrac{5}{6} = \dfrac{30}{36}$
2.) $\dfrac{10}{12} = \dfrac{5}{6}$
3.) $\dfrac{2}{6} = \dfrac{1}{3}$
4.) $\dfrac{2}{4} = \dfrac{12}{24}$
5.) $\dfrac{1}{5} = \dfrac{3}{15}$
6.) $\dfrac{4}{5} = \dfrac{24}{30}$
7.) $\dfrac{3}{6} = \dfrac{15}{30}$
8.) $\dfrac{2}{5} = \dfrac{4}{10}$
9.) $\dfrac{1}{4} = \dfrac{6}{24}$
10.) $\dfrac{6}{12} = \dfrac{1}{2}$

Exercise No. 28

1.) $\dfrac{6}{36} = \dfrac{1}{6}$
2.) $\dfrac{3}{4} = \dfrac{6}{8}$
3.) $\dfrac{4}{10} = \dfrac{2}{5}$
4.) $\dfrac{3}{9} = \dfrac{1}{3}$
5.) $\dfrac{12}{24} = \dfrac{3}{6}$
6.) $\dfrac{3}{4} = \dfrac{15}{20}$
7.) $\dfrac{12}{20} = \dfrac{3}{5}$
8.) $\dfrac{2}{5} = \dfrac{8}{20}$
9.) $\dfrac{12}{16} = \dfrac{3}{4}$
10.) $\dfrac{1}{4} = \dfrac{2}{8}$

www.ingramcontent.com/pod-product-compliance
Lightning Source LLC
LaVergne TN
LVHW061322060426
835507LV00019B/2263